SPORTY
SPICE
IN MY POCKET

MEL C

B⊡XTREE

First published in the UK in 1997 by Boxtree,
an imprint of Macmillan Publishers Ltd, 25 Eccleston Place, London,
SW1W 9NF and Basingstoke

Associated companies throughout the world

ISBN 0 7522 1158 7

Text © 1997 Boxtree

Photographs: All Action – front & back cover, 1, 3, 11, 13, 14, 17, 21, 31,
33, 34, 36, 40, 43 Capital Pictures – 4, 9, 18 & 19, 22 & 23, 24 & 25, 28,
44 & 45, 48 Retna – endpapers, 6, 26 & 27, 39, 47

9 8 7 6 5 4 3 2 1

A CIP catalogue record for this book is available from the
British Library

Design by Blackjacks

Concept by Clare Hulton

Printed in Singapore

Neither the members of the Spice Girls nor any of their representatives
have had any involvement with this book.

Full name:
Melanie Jayne Chisholm

Date of birth: 12 January 1976

Distinguishing marks:
Two tattoos on right arm

Height: 5ft 6in

SPORTY SPICE LOVES DAMON ALBARN FROM BLUR WHO SHE THINKS ARE 'THE BEST BAND IN THE WORLD'

'I'M VERY DETERMINED. I THINK I CAN BE A BIT ANNOYING, BUT I'M GLAD I'M LIKE THAT. I DON'T THINK I'M A GREAT SINGER, BUT I LOVE IT.'

MEL C HAS A WEAKNESS FOR CHINESE FOOD

ALTHOUGH SHE APPEARS CONFIDENT, SPORTY SPICE CLAIMS TO BE VERY SHY. SHE'LL DO ANYTHING ON STAGE BECAUSE IT'S NOT THE SAME AS A ONE-TO-ONE ENCOUNTER

GERI SAYS THAT MEL C CAN SOMETIMES BE A BIT TOO STRAIGHT-LACED: ALL HER JEANS ARE FOLDED THE SAME WAY AND SHE HATES NOT GETTING ENOUGH KIP

MEL C LEFT HER HOME IN WIDNES, MERSEYSIDE, TO STUDY BALLET AND JAZZ IN KENT

SPORTY SPICE WOULD RATHER PLAY FOOTBALL THAN WATCH ROMANTIC FILMS - SHE BELIEVES THAT FOOTBALL IS EXTREMELY PASSIONATE

WHEN THE SPICE GIRLS TURNED ON THE OXFORD STREET 1996 CHRISTMAS LIGHTS MEL C WAS SO MOVED THAT SHE CRIED!

MEL C ONCE WORKED IN A FISH AND CHIP SHOP!

SMOKING AND RUDE PEOPLE ARE TWO OF SPORTY SPICE'S PET HATES

SPORTY SPICE IS FOOTBALL CRAZY! SHE HAS A LIVERPOOL F.C. SEASON TICKET AND PLAYS FOR A WOMEN'S FOOTBALL TEAM ... WHEN SHE HAS TIME!

IN THE 'SAY YOU'LL BE THERE' VIDEO SPORTY SPICE'S CHARACTER WAS CALLED KATRINA HIGHKICK

MEL C IS KNOWN AS THE MOTHER HEN OF THE SPICE GIRLS - AND THE PEACEMAKER IN THE GROUP

MEL C CONFESSES TO OWNING TWO BRUCE WILLIS ALBUMS

SPORTY SPICE'S MUM AND STEP-DAD ARE ALSO IN SHOW BUSINESS. THEY BELONG TO A BAND CALLED T-JUNCTION

'BROOKSIDE' IS ONE OF MEL C'S FAVOURITE PROGRAMMES — THE SCOUSE ACCENTS MAKE HER FEEL BETTER WHEN SHE'S HOMESICK

SPORTY SPICE BELIEVES A GOOD FRIENDSHIP IS BETTER THAN A BOYFRIEND... BECAUSE IT WILL LAST FOR EVER

WHAT'S THE MOST SUCCESSFUL WAY TO CHAT UP SPORTY SPICE? INVITE HER ON A DATE TO A FOOTIE MATCH!

MEL C WAS ONCE BANNED FROM A GYM IN JAPAN BECAUSE OF HER TATTOO! IN JAPAN TATTOOS ARE ASSOCIATED WITH GANGSTERS AND THEY THOUGHT THAT SPORTY SPICE WAS A MEMBER OF THE MAFIA!